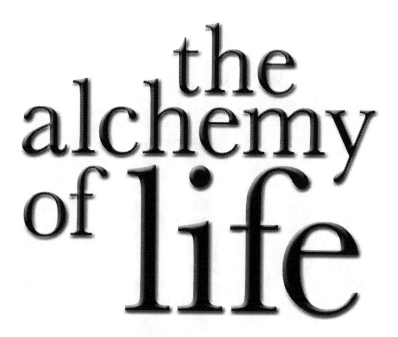

the alchemy of life

ALLYN BOUCHER

BALBOA.
PRESS

A DIVISION OF HAY HOUSE

Balboa Press books may be ordered through booksellers or by contacting:

Balboa Press
A Division of Hay House
1663 Liberty Drive
Bloomington, IN 47403
www.balboapress.com
1 (877) 407-4847

Because of the dynamic nature of the Internet, any web addresses or links contained in
this book may have changed since publication and may no longer be valid. The views
expressed in this work are solely those of the author and do not necessarily reflect the
views of the publisher, and the publisher hereby disclaims any responsibility for them.

The author of this book does not dispense medical advice or prescribe the use of any
technique as a form of treatment for physical, emotional, or medical problems without the
advice of a physician, either directly or indirectly. The intent of the author is only to offer
information of a general nature to help you in your quest for emotional and spiritual well-
being. In the event you use any of the information in this book for yourself, which is your
constitutional right, the author and the publisher assume no responsibility for your actions.

Any people depicted in stock imagery provided by Thinkstock are models,
and such images are being used for illustrative purposes only.
Certain stock imagery © Thinkstock.

Print information available on the last page.

ISBN: 978-1-5043-8050-8 (sc)
ISBN: 978-1-5043-8077-5 (e)

Library of Congress Control Number: 2017907596

Balboa Press rev. date: 06/02/2017

acknowledgements

there are two people to whom I owe special gratitude of thanks. one is my beautiful niece Laura, who singlehandedly gave me the courage to express to the whole world what I was feeling. my writing was always so intensely personal that I dared not share my secrets. through Laura I learned that everybody has such secrets, and I'm no exception to the involved brooding. Laura validates my feelings and fully applauds who I am.

the other person responsible is my friend, LuLu Richardson, whom people recognize as a bright light in Unity Of Birmingham. once I got accustomed to Laura reading my writing, I became more and more open about my feelings. LuLu provided the platform for me to share my writings with the people of Unity of Birmingham.

this little book is dedicated to you both!

with lots of love and blessings,

Allyn Boucher

prologue

the disconnect between who we are and who we force ourselves to play like on the earth causes us so much pain and slavery.

the smart ones learn their assignments quickly, and early, and then later they may spend good money trying to rearrange their learned false lessons, and capture the truth.

but when one has a friend, a true, unequivocal friend, who mirrors back the truth, and can peel away the layers of deceit, without guilt or judgment or manipulation, then is that one fortunate and blessed, for in that way a path is provided, a way home, to return to that which we are, that which we've always longed to be, which is that which we already are.

for me, that friend is this writing.

living with nothing and no one against us

entering Holy Ground – seeking nothing but everything – which is within us at all times –
    we present ourselves at this portal.

the alchemy we put to active use has left us whole, refreshed,
    and has successfully transmuted our chains of ignorance into the
    feather-lightness of Wisdom and Truth.

the dimension of darkness that was with us for so long has now been excused –
    our hearts have been unleashed and we can breathe.

we are the answers, and we know this Path – it is carved in our souls.

we know the Grace - it has sustained and upheld us for eons.

we are invited to the feast which is set before us and we are blessed in unimaginable ways.

we tread lightly over this terrain of Love, for our feet are held and caressed
    by the angel hands that have been with us from the beginning.

we do not have to muzzle our laughter or joy at the magnificence
    of this time.

we have been drawn through the eye of the needle into the
    fullness of ourselves,

the dark night is subsiding and in its place – sanctuary.

    serenity is ours for the taking.

our assignment now is to enjoy That which we have and are,

and to simply allow our unfoldment in the Love of God.

come – let us play innocently in this unspeakable Field of Light!

the soft, lush green of the earth melts beneath my footstep. carefully crafted paths of the past fall away, and I find I am alone in the deep forest. dreams and goals that I once thought worthy crumble to crust in my hand and tumble to the ground.

now, to breathe.

silence. solace. stillness. I am welcome here.

but it is so dark, so damp, so cold. I feel lost, agonized about the apparent separation, confused. and I think for a moment that I have lost my way.

searching for sanctuary, for help, I breathe once again. I cry out and scream and beg for mercy. No response. I cry louder, and the lack of response is all the louder.

and so, I give up, and sit down to drink my despair. and breathe.

and breathe.

and breathe.

then, something from within.

I begin to recognize all that I am, and it brings me untold comfort. like a rush. of something good.

it's as though a warm, velvet blanket is lovingly placed on my shoulders—and yet, I am naked here in these woods. and now, no longer alone, I am surrounded by the whole host of heaven whose angel wings brush up against my throat and hover over my heart.

the tortuous, deceptive shackles of the past are crushed beneath the feathers and tossed into ashes for the earth's digestion. betrayers are brought before me and forgiven, one by one. evil bows at my feet and is transmuted into love and set free at my hand.

and although I came into this forest in seeming darkness and cold, seeking only escape from the pain,

in my desolation I encountered the truth and the wealth within, and am saved by my own soul. and heaven and earth are mine, and all the treasures of the universe.

the universe is purring again. this is not the first time, and won't be the last. all of the outlaws will soon succumb to her majesty, and be still. we will all be still. shhhhh...

she beckons me lately. but it is summer, and I don't visit my woods in the summer, and the yard is not the same. yet, she calls to me.

now I realize—she is within me, and that is what is calling. it isn't the fairies and elves that want me to come out and play, it is my own self, my own goddess. listen.

the subtleties and nuances of the moon-cast shadows dance just outside of my reach. they flirt with my heart, yet I have nothing to worry about. my breath is wide. it encompasses all that I can see and spills over the edges of the earth. it is warm and safe and still. there is nowhere to go, and nothing to get.

the journey has seemed long and very arduous, but in the eyes of some it has been but an instant. it all depends on perspective and vision.

vision. how we see results in what we see. what did I see? sometimes something short of perfection. sometimes something I wish to reject. but now I am changing that, because I can. because I want to, and because I can.

goddess. I am indeed. and the goddess that I am rises up within me and seizes her pen and paper and comes to this table to write. she picks up the tools on the ledge and recognizes each one as hers. she knows when and how to use them each as she silently beckons her own power. the air begins to quiet above her, and the forces of the fire subdue under her thought. she inhales the truth within her lungs and lets it circulate in the universe that is her body, her temple. she exhales the transmuted forces of love and good and light and they spill like waters on the face of the earth. they quench all thirst and resurrect all hopelessness into wisdom. she watches as evil is softened and darkness is excused. and she knows. she breathes again. and she knows. she knows. she knows.

the Center of the Universe drops into the depths of my Heart.

I silence my mind, hush my throat and go there.

it is quiet. and still. the air feels damp and cool. it drifts over my skin and seeks my lungs where it finds pleasure.

the quieter I become, the richer I am.

it builds slowly, but surely, as the tortoise to the finish.

there is no hurrying this, but then, I don't wish to. there is no need for rushing.

time ceases to matter here, and that is welcome peace to my perception of the hastening society around me.

Wisdom matters, that's what. Wisdom, and Love.

and Love is here. the Love that creates worlds and people and hope and joy.

and there is nowhere to go, nothing to get.

nowhere.

nothing.

and so I sit still, and just breathe......

we line our own path with nails and broken glass then we complain about the pain –

shhhh......... for a moment.........

this is about redemption, salvation – the christian's favorite topics.

but there's a thief within who would rather put the mark of the beast on our heart, than
    reciprocate the silence,

and it's politics as usual as long as you keep moving.

so, stop. still. and.........

...we are invited to inject the chemistry of our magic into the alchemy of our souls, to breathe
    in the balance and exchange it for our fear,

and then the good news is that we are free...

and the bad news is, that we are free.

the goddess leans into the wind. she licks her lips, closes her eyes, and listens.

in the dark silence of the morning, she once again hears the Truth –

that there is nowhere to go and nothing to get.

satisfied, she blesses all within her sight,

and rises to meet the rush of Day.

the goddess stirs and shifts.

the magic within her is ignited and her spirit moves.

she is now being introduced to an even greater Truth – higher –

she allows the tantalizing effects to beckon her further, deeper, closer, than ever before.

her keen eyes watch, and listen – her supple heart purrs in her soul,

in her graciousness and benevolence she stops to scoop up the whole world in her arms,
    to carry them with her on this journey,
        and finds that they are feather-light and the road becomes.
all the more powerful, and enticing…

in the dark silence, she breathes.

her powerful path is lined with ethers of soft clover, cottony and warm.

her big heart is invited to ease into the infinity of the moment, and she dances into the circle
of light cast around her.

the goddess moves gently through the powerful earth, carrying light in her belly,
    the elementals seek her out.
there is no time here – she rules the present, she owns this earth, there is no fear.
the absence of fear breeds patience, and the intelligent wisdom unfolds.
the idea of evil is a simple amusement since harm cannot exist without breath.
nor venom, without the fang.

breathe. be still. and silent.

let the rich wealth of the Truth drift over you.

let it wash you in the pristine Love that you are.

let it yield to you all that you need, all that you ask for, all that you see,

    all that would serve you.

let it bring you freedom from dis-ease, struggle and poverty of every kind.

let it comfort you. let it guide you. let it deliver wisdom at every turn.

let it be. for that is what is before us – to allow the handsome Truth to BE.

a dark and stormy earth moved across the face of the moon last night.

she seemed sullen and pouty. so I went out to talk with her, to see if I could transmute her ill mood…

she is my friend, my companion, my confidante and my home.

and so, I approached her as such.

and she quickly saw my sincerity and entrusted me with her deepest soul,

and this is what she said.

"I have not been treated well by your kind, yet do I love you, still. but things are rapidly changing now, and will continue to do so for a while. seeds have been sown that are reaping a harvest, so be wise. and be cautious. listen deeply to your own souls now, seek refuge within – for there truly is nowhere to go and nothing for you to get, but what you must do to negotiate this next turn in the road will come from your own internal map, your own internal GPS, if you will. if you listen to yourself and heed what your own guidance tells you, you will be fine. and I do not intend to couch any of this in threatening terms. quite the contrary. but I want you to know that the Wisdom and Guidance that you need, and that you will need, you have. it is within you, even now, even as you write these words. where do you think this conversation is coming from? yes. you are correct. it is coming from you, from YOU, for you are not separate from He/She Who creates all things, moment by moment.

"so. go on for now, be with yourself – deeply – and listen to yourself, and follow your own guidance. and the satisfaction that is returned to you from doing such will carry you and elevate you to a high place of safety, surrounded and drenched in love and light."

…and so it is, and so I let it be. and I am grateful, grateful, great-full.

the guide-dog from Hades has now arrived to discuss the day's gloom.

he is welcome here.

clearly, he knows this path well and is

    prone to helping those who would take his leash.

he is neither proud nor stubborn,

    and he seeks no reward for his aid.

in a moment's hesitation, we can observe the universe turning in soft silence,

we can ingest the thoughts of 10,000 souls, dark or light.

in one moment's receptivity we can receive all the answers to the prayers of infinity,

    and be gifted with birth or death.

in one moment of time we can stop time and become the rulers that we are.

or we can step off into the madness known by others.

in one moment a blink can restore all forgiveness and innocence

    and transmute our fears, or it can not, and we lose the treasure of the moment.

in one, limitless moment,

all can be ours.

the insincerity of 10,000 vulgar cheats taunts my better senses tonight.

they all smile and nod and say "I do" on election's eve,

but in the morning they go about slinking through their slimy hours

    thinking how they can cheat us all

of that which is ours and keep it for themselves.

they play their games and pin the tail on the donkey of the day and then

    go out and regain those very same votes all over again when

once more we are presented with an opportunity for Truth,

    or something like it.

our choices are limited and they slide from bad to worse.

this is not democracy. it's hypocrisy.

I'd best keep to myself the next few days.......

14

the quiet dove tucks her wing and feathers her heart.

she prints the earth with sound and waits for that which she is.

her authority settles the lawlessness of nations and

her decency delivers revenge.

with perfect courtesy she forgives the enmity of her neighbors and becomes in a moment
their idol.

her jurisdiction is nothing less than life itself,
from which she retrieves perfect beneficence.

her purchase is perfection, and she hovers over sin, watching for the perfect strike.

at the moment that timelessness is hers and order is restored,

she lets go the talon's leash

and waves her spell of peace upon the hungry earth.

breathe. drink the wind.

what my soul longs for

is that which it already owns.

the forfeiture of freedom passes like a shadow

before my closed eyes.

    open.

there's Truth to be had for the taking. free for all who come to the fold.

salvation is not the property of the devil.

    it is ours.

16

the impact of the souls pressed hard in on the Truth.

there was no way it could evaporate now.

they had it in their hands.

the elusive beauty of it slowly seeped forth.

a sheet of ice covered the mouths of the demons who would deny the goodness of this.

the thing was set in motion – it had begun.

and so, a grain of light found its mate,

and together they seized the eyes of one, and became a third.

and then that one, and the next and the next and on and on and on and on until –

…until one day the woman became the earth's,

the child became the air,

and the word was born.

there is so much......

with swift and cunning eloquence the leopard bears down on me with his singular gifts.

his holy fangs offer to deliver me from evil

    and restore my soul.

with his wisdom to guide me we will move to higher ground,

and leave the others to play in the quagmire, if that is what they so choose.

    as for me?

I'd rather play among the living than the dead

and enjoy the incense of salvation and

discuss the elements of Truth with this leopard.

a frozen leaf outside the window seemed falling earthward, but then it stopped.

it betrayed gravity's force and paused, as if to review its choices.

for long enough it stayed that way, in mid-air, that I thought it still tethered to the tree.

    but slowly then it fell, and

I heard soft laughter as it kissed the tawny earth.

the monarch has arrived with his construction crew.

the plentiful supplies have been spread out, blanketing infinity.

a demon child who arrived with bloody hands has now been transmuted into an age of innocence, and has ascended to the throne of wisdom and peace.

and the good Truth Remains inextinguishably Rich, while genuine poverty abounds, in the delusions of the still confused.

the breath of life has been breathed into my hungry nostrils, and my cowering heart has been irresistibly invited to the inquisition.

I face my captors.

they stand before me with open hand, holding out the key to their prison door.

reluctantly, weepingly, I took it from them this morning, the key they offered. they wanted me to take it, they wanted me to be free.

they have no complaint about the threshold I have reached and in fact they encouraged me to walk forward into the center within.

I am the wistful one, wishing somewhat to stay in the delusional fairytale so long in my bones, afraid to bring down the dynasty, their dynasty. but, it is time to move through all of this. they want me to dust off the inaccuracies and bring forth the fullness of my presence - and so do I.

they handed me my leash and told me they did not want it anymore, that it was not theirs to carry, and it belonged to me. I knew that taking it from them would change everything. but I knew that I must –

that is.. ...if I want to frolic with the Truth and align myself with the Sun and the Moon and the Stars.

it is a choice.

the woods are rich and lovely these days.

bare limbs beckon me fill their little branches with my thoughts of the day and poetry.

today they were especially enticing. the wind cruised overhead, running its bony fingers through the pine trees, sweeping the sky with this swoosh.

I always stop what I'm doing whenever I hear the wind in the pines, to drink that lonely ache that comes over me, even if for a moment, and to salute one of my favorite items in nature. it is a singularly worthy thing.

Sanctuary.

it is here, now, and I entered its holy walls and sat down for some much-welcome salve.

and already, the scented balm oozes toward my heart.

the chair that was her beloved resting place, is now my beloved cocoon, and I treasure its gifts every one, for they are powerful and encompassing and no thief can snatch them from their worth.

and I have with me of course my priest and confessor, and my hand is ready to seek the deity of my talents.

sanctuary.

finally.

at last.

the manuscript we are given I'm told is of our own writing, and I've no reason to doubt that.

but how far back do we reach when we seek the reasons for our Karma, and how far forward can we leapfrog over our own past?

good questions, both, whose answers may not be translatable to the page.

the agony that befell me this weekend took my passion for the day.

it sponsored its own brooding demons and it left me bound and gagged.

the rashness with which it descended sent my otherwise perfect words to the floor, and left me in its unfriendly jurisdiction.

the only one who benefitted from my mood were those who love evil, and myself, for in the end I was restored to my own timeless art and I was able to float above the incomplete defeat.

and in the end I was able to remember my list of ingredients and duplicate the Road to salvation.

but it was hell before I got there.

the writer's paw beckoned early this morning, to excuse all the sins and superficialities of the day before.

the now merger that was carefully crafted just recently has yielded exciting peace and prosperity.

i sit here now within the perfect world, and covet that which I already have.

the dark and the light that have slaughtered so many efforts have now shown the flawlessness of their intent, and I am free to embrace as much of all their goodness as my hungry belly can hold.

it is with time that all things come to pass.

and although we are told that time is an artificial construct for man's life on earth, it is still difficult to avoid its fencing.

in time we grow and learn, whether now to love and be to our fullest or how to curse the soil and set ourselves back with greed.

in time the benevolent processes of life wrap gently through our cells, and we learn to breathe and give and forgive and ingest the salvation of our gifts.

it is with time that we lick the wounds of grief and watch the bleeding stop, leaving whatever scar of remembrance is required, while yet closing the gap once found in the flesh of our hearts.

and it is in time, and honred with crystal opportunities, that I myself am able to once more befriend my own soul in these pages, and be where I so love to be – right here, right now.

in a small, dark corner of the earth, light in seedling form brews silently.

it is watched over by hummingbirds and guarded by the fallen feathers of owls.

man has laughed at its seeming weakness and has therefore shunned its offerings, choosing instead the forceful industry.

but all the creatures of earth's forests, and all the magical creatures who dwell on the unseen planes know the power and mystery of this infant goodness, and so they forfeit their own days and years to see its safekeeping.

it is not something any one of them can carry on their backs, nor something to be held in their paws, but they tremble with joy at the knowledge that its truth is imparted to them for their recognition, and can never be taken from them.

and I, too, have been there and seen it, and I, too, have joined in its following.

and in exchange I have transmuted fear into hope, and death into power and peace.

the art of living life is a terribly beautiful thing.

so often tormented souls are tempted beyond resistance to terminate the gift, feeling its compensations do not sufficiently pay its debts.

but now these days I read of ever new hope on the horizon, and very nearly upon us, indeed.

the very failures of the Lord of Creation are shown to be perfect success.

the defeat and shadow that have darkened so many hearts is transmuted into victory itself.

the signs may well indicate some good change is impending, some welcome composition for our eyes and ears and souls.

the Revolution may very well be on its way, just as surely as the evolution of us all.

and the sins of the fathers that have been visited on the sons will be substituted for intelligence and wisdom.

the intellect of mankind will encompass compassion for all of life, and healthy animals will be allowed to live.

the moisture that has gathered will lead to a River of Love and Light.

there has been a sufficient amount of absence lately that my stomach is growling to be fed.

the confetti of life clogs the filters so often and we find we only see so little.

our once-pure vision is slowly exchanged for imitation and the news is ingested as truth.

but I am told of another list, one kept carefully by the Lord of the Universe and perfectly calibrated for the answers.

and the lawyer within me who perfectly argues his case to the jury leaves me speechless with the knowledge of the truth.

once today I wandered through the sins of others, and saw their artless pain inflicted on the innocent creatures of heaven, and I think my heart took a permanent turn.

for so long now, slowly realizing I no longer want to plunk high dollars down on a perfect specimen or other, now I know that those same dollars I would rather choose to put some previous stepchild in high cotton.

high dollars for high cotton.

I have no grudge for those flawless puppies others put on the earth one by one, but I want the cast-offs now.

I say let them know my couch and my bed and my love.

let them be mine, and godspeed the others find their own perfect homes, which I am sure they will.

now just a short space for the taking, tempting my thoughts to be succinct. easy to do, no problem: the angel perseveres and stubbornly pursues the plans of God.

there is no conversation that is not worth having with her, for she leads me to the only worthy worship.

and so, we go.

she knows me, and she has come to Rescue the Rescuer.

it is a recurrent theme: the fingers of Existence leave us weary and alone, and we forget the very reason that we came.

the compositions in our lives but duplicate themselves in unsatisfactory manner, and so we seek comfort elsewhere.

in thoughtless adoration we create our molten gods and the more we sink the more we worship, simply driving our souls deeper into debt.

but sometimes we are either visited by an angel or locked in a prison of pain, and then we see the invitation, there, on the wall.

and it goes something like this: "the Truth is within. the Truth shall set you free. so be still, and Know."

33

So this morning my plan is just this: to sit and be. perhaps to write. to let my heart wander around in some good and purposeful thoughts, to munch quietly on some small but infinitely Expansive Treasure.

for so often—and increasingly so, I suspect—I have gotten caught up in the doings of life and have forfeited the simple value of being.

I see it all around me, indeed, its pervasiveness is hard to avoid. but so is its emptiness.

to be driven and driven, leaping from one pad to the next, ever searching for something we cannot even name, yet whose call haunts us day and night, like some primal instinct.

but we do not find it by our scurrying efforts.

though our very hand be on the latch of that door, we do not realize.

and so it goes.

but I keep coming back to the Knowledge that if I just stop running and performing with such effort, the effortlessness of my breath will yield the very security and peace and answer I seek.

for it is within.

force.

the force with which we live our lives takes form in a variety of ways.

sometimes we use our force for doing good deeds, for cursing disease or dispelling poverty and ignorance.

sometimes we direct our force poorly, into ways that hurt and haunt and will inevitably return to inflict some painful lessons on us in return.

and other times we spend our force in a restless wandering, exerting ourselves thoughtlessly on the world and our fellow man, while not listening deeply to the subtle pulse of the earth.

we flail and flaunt like fish out of water, and are darkly unaware of our own space in life.

I have more often than not been guilty of just such squandering of force, thrashing in the flow of life rather than drinking and digesting its gifts and opportunities.

but, I'm not done yet.

I'm still here.

and I'm reflecting on all this now.

so let me continue to ponder this wisdom and see if I might prefer a little different path from here, one which involves more trust in the process and more acknowledgment of the Truth.

the techniques of avoidance are betraying me now, and this is a bittersweet development.

I am growing weary of my lifelong games.

they wear thin, now, and no longer amuse me so much.

their tactics and temptations were fine for many years, and downright pleasurable in their path.

but the playthings of the past do not intrigue me as much these days as myself, and I find the hunt changing course, as the faithful rabbit completes its predictable circle and returns to that which is its own.

36

and again, the same theme.

the salvation within.

but what so often scalds my hands and frightens me to drop the enormous truth when I hold it close, is my own lack of control over it.

that is at once the greatest blessing, and for me, the greatest curse.

ah, how deeply I want to be able to earn it, to do something, to prove myself worthy and to receive my Oscar because of something I did or said or was.

to be that actress whose nomination justifiably Results in the award, because I was such a good girl.

but it can't be that way.

it isn't that way, I do not need it to be that way, and I certainly do not truthfully want it to be that way.

I'm only regurgitating that which I was taught, and which was modeled for me, but it isn't the good truth.

it is for Charlatans and tricksters and the troll under the bridge.

but for me, as for for me, perhaps I will finally marry and settle down with the alluring reality, and become obedient to its happy ways.

an ageless, timeless ache has befriended my bones tonight, not bones of the body, but of the heart.

an issue has been gently placed on my front step and the Provider rang the doorbell then vanished.

but I opened the door, and looked out at this thing, this uncertainty, and I took it inside by the fire.

and now that we are here where I can see clearly, I need to think.

the drawer that I slammed on my finger this morning has opened anew and asked me: what of this?

and I certainty don't have the answer right now. I know where to go to retrieve it, I just must be silent to receive it.

38

the aristocracy of true politics has left the actors speechless in their efforts to be still.

what once was bought and paid for is now free and easily within their reach.

it just seems so strange that it is that way, that most of them do not seize the opportunity.

but, it will come again, that chance.

quiet.

bone deep quiet.

still.

like the sound the earth makes as she revolves on her axis.

silent.

the stars, the moon.

they live and move and have their being, in utter speechlessness, our animals.

the whole Kingdom.

soundless, wordless.

so often I wonder what they would say, so often I wonder what they feel.

they can not tell me, and I can't always tell.

I wish I knew more what they think – I think.

40

my soul was crying this morning.

the deepest part of my heart wept openly, so that it stopped me in my tracks.

and once the initial slash tore open the pocket of ache within, it contrived to trickle but in blood-red droplets.

a chameleon sunrise befriended me and soothed my breakfast of pain.

I watched as it presented words of Rescue and Truth, and warned me heed its good promise.

there is magic going on in countless corners of the world, and increasingly so in some.

and there are as many different kinds of magic as there are people with eyes to see.

and there is no shortage of magic going on right here, and now, and within my own wingspan.

the aches and pains of life that yield decay for the forest floor, but provide the sustenance for resurrection when the dark night of inertia has ended.

and all these things that we think we don't know what to do, we do, or shall.

and just like sometimes the pen and paper betray me and do not deliver me peace, even when they do so, they have their purpose.

the golden-eyed chick is purring on her nest.

the opposition of ten thousand has not deterred her, nor kept her from the Truth.

the fearless secret that she laid before my table has ushered in an age of new becoming.

some once-mighty warriors last night beat their drums in her ear, and bid her betray her own peace.

they mocked her with their evil politics and spat on her unspoiled wealth.

but her power was not for sale or for bargain and her treasure is free for the taking.

and in the end she sent them away in speechless confusion when she said that goodness could not be bought or stolen, and that the key to its Resurrection was within.

some of them fainted on their feet, and some of them cursed in anger.

but some of them took her words home and tucked them under their own wings for later review.

and these were the ones who Returned to the fullness and wealth of timelessness.

today I invited the beckoning ghosts come dine at my table with me.

I fling open wide the doors of my heart and bid them feast on my aching wounds.

they entered in force, silently but closely, and they sat with me for a time in my car.

we wandered through a maze of timeless memories and shopped at the heartache for sale.

we drank deeply of each other's company – they knew they were asked to enter and showed no signs of nervousness.

and then, after a while, I waved them good bye, and explained that they must return to their drawer and sleep. so, they did.

obedient ghosts, they.

but later en route home, I became so sad, and I wept.

once here, I wandered through the woods and wondered, did I make a mistake to invite them out to play?

did I?

or, was I letting my soul the more deeply breathe and be where I really was?

was I simply uncorking an ageless wine, and letting it sigh forth its fenced-in vapors?

it's spring.

the relentlessly beautiful bird is commanding, non-stop, that all the earth listen to him and engage his being.

his cooperative policies are fascinating to the gods.

I can see they are awe-struck at his song.

he barely draws breath before he sings again, and nothing monotonous at that.

he rolls and rolls through infinite variety, sitting confidently alone.

but at this rate, he won't be alone long.

44

the 5th revised edition of life is winding its song through the earth.

in stripes of zebra black and white it lays its perfect plans down.

an infinite flock of geese gather to worship the thing that they know is the truth.

and even the clergy bow down now – if they are listening – for the idolatry of the past is transmuting into the path of the true present, and bedtime for delusion is upon us.

the sequel to life is presenting itself to my spirit.

its eloquent hum strokes gently in my ear.

the uncomfortable discontinuity with which we all were smitten has now succumbed to the beginning, and the harpists' fingers are on the latch.

a mushroom-colored mare whose tail circles the earth moved in to stand on my heart.

her hooves dispelled the disagreement of the demons and commanded their silent submission.

in perfect fashion the earth spins and moves and all the stars glide in obedience.

somehow, something is going to happen some day, and perhaps the minute pettiness that we mistook for such will have shown itself to be the miracle of infinity.

the soft and malleable part of the universe is mine these days.

the earth absorbs my footprint like the impression in a child's playdough, and only slowly and gradually reforms.

the tears of ancient heaven are at my fingertips, and the brooding dark of melancholy hovers overhead.

it is spring. there are many changes about.

birth is beautiful, but painful, and once the birthling is born, things will never be the same again, for good.

change.

it's all about change.

and the transformations of energy's subtle power yield both pleasure and pain, but it is a cycle that we can only watch.

if we are wise, we breathe in deeply and drink in the dark and the light and absorb the black sun into our skin.

and we learn to watch, and be patient.

if we are restless and young, our hearts may deceive us, and we may think we can outrun the earth's revolutions and hold the passage of time in our palm.

but we cannot do it that way, and eventually we will see that.

eventually we all will see that.

and then we will be where we want to be, which is just where we are.

the cycles of life that tug at our bones and place bread on our table cannot be peacefully ignored.

in the silence of our traffic jam our own spiritual vomit will creep out to be heard at some point, if we refuse to listen.

we artificialize our routines and we hasten to disenjoy each moment only to find the sun has risen and it's time to start all over.

but, I caught a glimpse of something different: to cease fighting the cycles, to live within nature's realm, to breathe in synch with the ebb and flow, the dark and light, and to be that which we really are, rather than that which we force ourselves into.

to live and move and have our being within the warm, eternal womb of truth, and to relinquish our death grip on the dissention in our souls, and fall into the skillful rescue of eternity, and truth.

my, what peace we would savor then, and what celebration of comfort

the earth kissed me with a dark, wet kiss this morning.

the simplest thing to do is to be and yet the being eludes my present moment too often, and makes my spirit weary.

in the running hither and yon, we often lose sight of the purpose of life and we cease to reflect.

as such, we fail to tend our garden and we watch as weeds run rampant.

simple droplets of blood ooze quietly from her cheeks.

verdant green eyes seethed with fire, questioning.

in a melancholy cocoon she wrapped her silver spoon,

and sat beside the moon for conversation.

"how are you," she asked, knowing full well the moon was not the same since man stepped upon her.

"doing as well as can be expected," came the obvious reply.

and then they sat in silence, holding hands, looking inward, reflecting on one another's burdens and joys and on the plight assigned them.

the snowcapped mountain of ten thousand wounded souls has melted to the forest floor.

the citizens of the earth are haunted, and searching, but hopeful.

they cast their nets to the sea, and bring back 5 loaves and 2 fishes.

once they turn to mend their nets, the fishes have become limitless, and the supply is never-ending.

a dark, velvet depth has lain ice in my heart these recent weeks, and I have been cheated by the pauper's prayer.

my soul was torn from its rightful throne of love, and is in my hand, counterfeit coins of worthless use.

I ached for sight, to be able to see, because I was so undeniably blinded by the assault that sliced my eyes.

groping, feeling my way, awash in horror and disbelief, I was completely unprepared for the poison that defiled my innocent laughter and drove me to the ground.

but, slowly, the hand reached down for me and slowly, slowly, it pulled me out of the slump.

not in an instant, nor the blink of an eye, for remember time passes so tediously when one is lost in the quicksand.

but still, it came.

the good truth peeked out, like some newborn sliver of grass whose spring has finally come.

and things began to rearrange, and the sage took my arm and guided me past the dirt.

and now here I stand with my present in my hand and the pen and paper at the ready and I know more now than I did before these recent weeks of mine.

the lenient forgiveness of the priestess is mine.

She knew of my vicious wickedness before I even shed a tear.

and She waited.

She planted her holy hand on the scroll and counted the ashes that fell from my heart.

She locked in on my Soul with her placid eyes of grey and let her breath rise and fall with all of Nature's rhythm.

She never begged or pleaded, She never manipulated or cursed me.

She just waited.

and while she did so my hand was quietly sitting, searching for the seam between the dark and the light, resting fitfully on my lap, writing sometimes and finding some answers, but so often wondering how to hold my life.

but she was always there, always here, and always courteous and generous with her wisdom and Truth.

a welcome ride through the woods today on my buttermilk-colored horse.

he carried me eagerly, impatient to resume our ongoing dialogue with the elementals, determined to speak with each one in turn and satisfy himself as to their status.

the woods have now bloomed verdant and full for the summer, their radar at capacity to seek the summer owls.

the trees are all laden with the baggage which will later provide gifts to the soil below them, and the warmth of the equator is closer, and it is good.

a solid velvet shawl draped loosely over her bony shoulders.

the dignity with which she held her court was undeniably rich.

with silk-like ease she conversed sincerely with all the paupers and priests who had sold a share of their hearts to be near her.

in timeless graciousness she blessed them all just to be near them, and they received their sought-after satisfaction.

the goodness was theirs, for simply having received her gifts, and for breathing in her presence.

no pressure. just kindness.

the midnight madness is momentarily excused.

the hounds of hell are quieted now by my own magic touch.

the earth continues in its rotary path, the sun and moon still dance along, but for now, all the Universe is mine, and I plan to spend it wisely.

the demons of yesterday have been temporarily excused.

they know their place, despite their snarl, and they know they'd best be silent.

the winds are mine today.

the earth and the rains wait patiently for me, willing to beg infinity to hush, to hear what it is I want.

everything is poured out before me and all I have to do is open my mouth to be fed.

the darkness.

I turn my back on the blind darkness, and sit quietly in the sanctuary.

the pews are slowly filling, as others trickle in.

the blissful smell of myrrh fills my room and perfect atonement radiates.

the elegant, sensuous perfection of Truth is quickly and quietly moving in, bringing the most delicious news.

it is not something to be bargained or sold, this cherishment.

and yet I say, on account of the flawless Truth, all debts are paid, and receipts are in hand.

the face of exaltation wraps 'round my startled hand just to steady it as I drop my cup of sin to the floor and see the pens of guilt shattered.

this is no mere frivolity.

this is Goodness and Salvation wrapped firmly in the twine of infinity and sealed with the kiss of unqualified freedom.

the uncanny paws of wealth have tramped all through my garden heart and sequestered my soul.

now we sit staring at each other, eye to eye, and I simply have nothing to say.

spell-bound, I nonetheless glide through my days as if something forever has changed, and I go about my business with the security of a millionaire.

I have everything I ever wanted to have, right here, right now.

and I wouldn't change a thing.

it is now.

the infinite rebirth of the soul is present.

we emerge from the dark womb of water and are gently placed on the earth.

our feet fumble and find the path, our hands grope and then are still, as our eyes open and adjust to the light we have brought with us.

the hounds of hell that for a long time kept morning at bay have retreated to their dens. their job is done.

we had to wait until we were ready to be with who we are but now is the time, and the union of light and dark, evil and good, birth and death, ignorance and wisdom, is here, perched on my palm, as man's intercession bleeds all the universe into One.

it is a sumptuous feast, this.

the edition of life in which I am engaged offers endless opportunity to nibble on the edges of Truth until our bellies can hold more.

and in the process of consumption we are renewed again and again and again, ever arriving closer to our true selves and embracing our own wealth.

I don't write poetry.

I don't write prose.

I write about the incongruous relationship we often create with ourselves and others and our world, in which we invite demons and shun our own freedom.

we breed misery and anger as frivolously and carelessly as if such did not matter.

we carry our delusions like a torch and walk away from comfort.

we seek our padded cells and scream out in horror, throwing ourselves from wall to wall and splattering our hearts.

then sometimes when we reach a point of choice, some flickering faint lightning begging to offer us a way out of our own created hell, we slam shut the door and wrap ourselves in deeper cold.

and we think we are right, and in just that moment, we are so wrong, and so we contact the abyss of our own self-made darkness.

…it's just that, visiting with ourselves, with who we are, sometimes at the end of a work day seems demanding.

odd, isn't it?

and yet it is so – we busy ourselves through the day with the tasks before us, and shifting years can be difficult.

so it's easier to ignore ourselves and stay on the track laid before us.

a blue-gray dawn visits early.

the satisfactions of the day before have left their pleasant smell on my skin, and brought me early to my senses this morning.

the visit with a messenger of light and love yesterday was more welcome than rain in the desert, and her thorough ministry to all my entities was received with perfect timing.

the refreshment of my soul was surprisingly overdue, and deeply welcome.

and the food for thought that she left on my plate is enticing and exciting and hopeful.

I want to be still, and quiet, and reflective, and to feed at the rich trough before me.

these days I witness a harvest of pain and struggle one hour, and the repose of anger the next.

the earth bakes its crusty soil in the sun's oven, and the animals endure the day's heat in stillness, as tails swish to chase the flies.

the summer is quite fully upon us now, and I see myself withdraw from the creative womb to wait.

I move through my days and nights with sufficient energy but for some reason the fullness of the earth dispels my creative hand, and I stare at nothing.

but it's O.K. this is part of the cycle, and I know: when the sun tilts away from us and the leaves begin to fall, my thirst for the pen will be stirred and this book shall cease to be such a stranger.

days and weeks and years have passed lately, and still we plod along.

my own spirit has been in ten thousand places, all within an hour, from mountain top to valley and in every shade of grey.

lost, I have felt lost, and lost from what I do not know.

shaken, and thrilled, knowledgeable, and stripped, and it has all been tossed in the air like confetti to fall slowly to the ground and be trampled underfoot.

oh, but wait! when the trampling occurs it returns items to the earth, where they soak and bubble and brew.

and then, when time is right, new things are brought forth, good things, and the Easter Resurrection has its way, frolicking over death.

but then, death is not such a bad thing, either, you know?

and now, some sort of shift has flirted with me lately, has caught my eye.

as if I caught a glimpse of something that glittered in the sun.

I knew I saw it, I felt it on my mouth, I knew without question that it was something good. it was just unfamiliar, is all.

and it had to do with the Truthful embracing of my own self, and of the One within.

there is satisfaction there, where this Truth is, that glitters under the pile.

walking the little dogs this afternoon down by the barn, when there in the corner of the fence, a yellow balloon lay quietly on the ground.

a balloon.

a yellow balloon, sent from daddy, to me.

it was not there earlier today when I walked down by the barn with the babies for a mid-day walk, but it was there now.

a yellow balloon, from my daddy.

    thank you, daddy. Thank you, Lord of the Universe.

the breath of life has been breathed into my hungry nostrils, and my cowering heart has been irresistibly invited to the inquisition.

I face my captors.

they stand before me with open hand, holding out the keys to their prison door.

reluctantly, weeping, I took it from them this morning – the key they held.

they wanted me to take it, they wanted me to be free.

they have no complaint about the threshold we have all reached, and in fact they encourage me to walk forward into the center within.

I am the wistful one, wishing somewhat to stay in the delusional fairytale so long in my bones, afraid to bring down the dynasty, their dynasty.

but, it is time to move through all of this, and anyway, they want me to.

they want me to cast off the inaccuracies and bring forth the fullness of my own true self.

and so do I.

and so, I began this morning, to do just that.

it's what we do in our minds, not in our hearts, that pulls us into the undertow.

in the verdant stillness of eternity, I am surrounded by wealth.

the Chalice of Life has been offered to me, placed gently before me, and

left there by God, for me to ponder.

through all the years of deriding it, of trashing, avoiding and misunderstanding it,

it sat quietly and patiently,

neither begging nor bargaining for me to come to the table.

waiting.

silent.

still.

...submitting no competition for the distractions that

glittered and flashed all around me.

and now............. here I am.

I have returned. I have come home to that which was always mine,

but whose unfathomable power and goodness frightened me.

I have come home to my own self, and I can think of no finer thing -

and yet,

the journey is just beginning.

it never ends.

in the cavernous echo of my own faint soul, I struggled, crawling, groping, lost.

the undertow of the vast dark that had drained my faith for so many weeks, seemed firmly in control, and I heard the demons of pain whispering and laughing at my own fear.

entrapped by confusion, uncertain of any element of salvation, I laid this darkness before you for discussion.

and with the strength and power of ten thousand, you ministered to my weeping soul, and beckoned me face the quenchless light and turn, and now I am once again enticed by the power within.

thank you.

there is a place that intrigues me.

in a quiet corner of the world, in cool, damp, evening air, in the unspeakable and limitless power of peace, where brute force is silenced and dissolved by lack of resistance.

there is a place, the place, of true power, and it is within.

it is within me.

it shuns artificial manipulation and sheds the insecurities born of delusion.

it has no time for cultivating low self-esteem or for honoring self-reproach.

its eye sees beyond all such deceit and wastes no more time there.

it is within me, it is mine, my place, and it is where I am to be found.

I'm going to spend more time there, as much time as I can, as much as it takes.

I love it here, in this crow's nest above the earth.

I can sit here and look straight out the door to mid-tree level, and watch as the earth slowly spins.

the virgin cotton softness oozes palpable warmth and folds its giant, gentle wings softly over my heart.

lately there have been things to celebrate, to ponder, and to digest.

right now there are more answers than questions, and the journey is enticing.

sometimes when I look up from my book the room seems foggy and unclear.

the shapes are easily discernable but the air in between them is murky.

I close my eyes and summon clarity, but that often does not change things.

and so I may return to my book, waiting it out, assuming that all is well and I am not really losing vision.

more words, more writing, more reflection, and time, and then I can look up again and see the clear air and count the molecules and I am left to wonder where the smoke went.

the fictional places that we sometimes create for ourselves do not serve us well.

we stomp and snort and bargain with the devil to avoid the very romance that life is.

we recount the darkness and turn our backs to the light and then we sleep in the pain we have embraced.

perhaps if we want we can do this instead:

we can frolic with the gods as we discover who we are;

we can drink from the well of kindness and sleep peacefully in the open air;

we can take ourselves by the hand and explore our unguarded selves, and find that the magic of the universe is within.

that sounds enchanting to me.

76

breathe.

breathe deeply.

be.

still.

the day is stretched before me and my heart stands at the ready to reflect.

my spirit is sufficiently receptive, my fingers nimble and willing.

breathe, deeply.

no less than the universe itself is waiting while i unfold my power.

the trunk inside has been dusted off, the dust of delusion dispelled.

i've long since opened it up to look in, to face demons and angels alike, and to command them both with my courage.

and lately i've begun to reach inside, to lay hands on the garment of power so neatly folded, and so long ago placed in the bottom of the lid shut tight and sealed by fear and misunderstanding.

but things are changing. something has changed.

and that which was so long taken from me has returned to its home in my heart.

that which is forfeited foolishly, to find something outside i believed better, has quietly crept back before me, holding in its hand the leash on my heart.

so now.

breathe. again.

because no less than the fullness of my own limitless power is at stake.

i am officially engaged in the process of letting that little girl out of the jar, and she is filled with a virulent force.

she is mine, she is me, and if i befriend her and make her mine, we two are one, boundless and wealthy.

i have been living with the alternative for many years now, and i know well, that unpleasant path.

77

words, words.

the dictionary is filled with words.

we want so painfully to "put our feelings into words" to contain them, to wrap them in packages, to present to others and receive them back, to reach out and bridge and convince ourselves that we are not alone, lonely as we are.

it's an understandable thing and an effort that has its merits as many beautiful words have been put together and have led to joy and understanding.

but the creatures we live with who do not share our words are no paupers of expression, without thesaurus or books.

perhaps we would do well to study their own mute intercourse and acknowledge the wealth of a look.

78

they came here on welcome terms but their actions quickly uninvited them.

they were to be guests, visitors, but they behaved as owners of this land.

they marked it with their ribbons and soiled it with their selfishness, and they left footprints to be erased.

what were they thinking? what did they want?

i surely do not know, but i do know this: they drove us to reclaim our rightful land and bar them from its borders.

their foolish act has severed a deal, and persuaded our privacy to resurface.

perhaps this is just as well. perhaps we need the space to ourselves.

it was long ago when i inherited the earth, that i sat on the footstool of heaven and delicately digested the ancient Truths of wisdom.

it was long ago, that my belly became full, that the Light that coursed through my bowels frightened away evil and whispered to angels, "come, closer."

it was my routine way to command heaven and earth, my effortless breath to set in motion the stars and the moon, and with the wink of an eye, send them to bed for the day.

and what of now?

have things changed?

no.

i only need to remember that which i am, and bring it to bear in the myriad challenges of all my personal daily activities.

that's all.